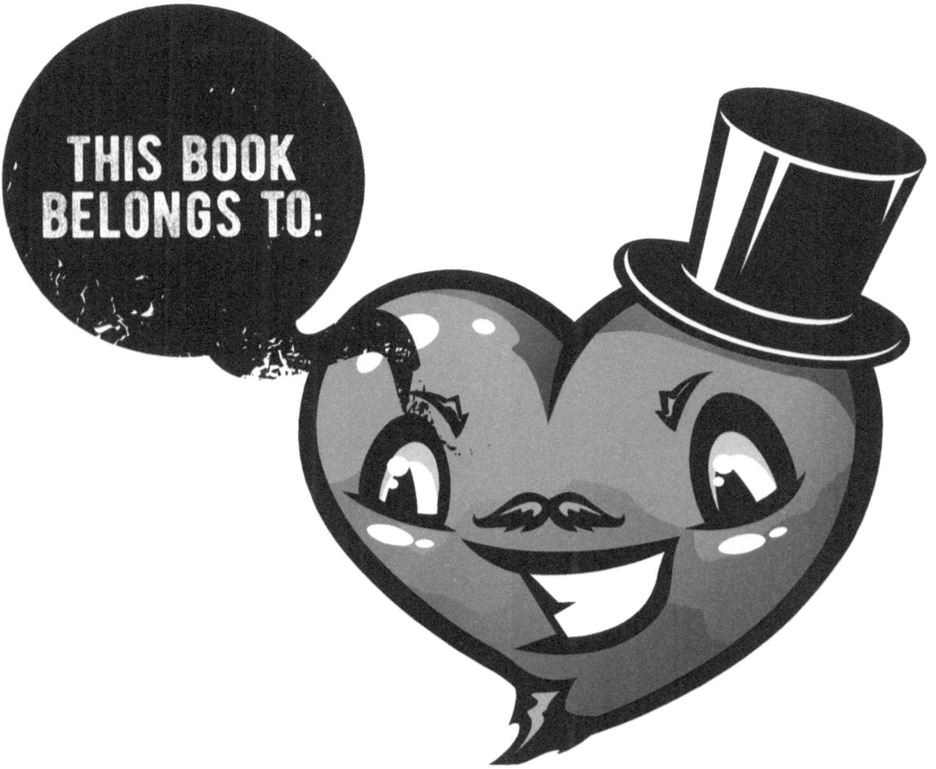
THIS BOOK BELONGS TO:

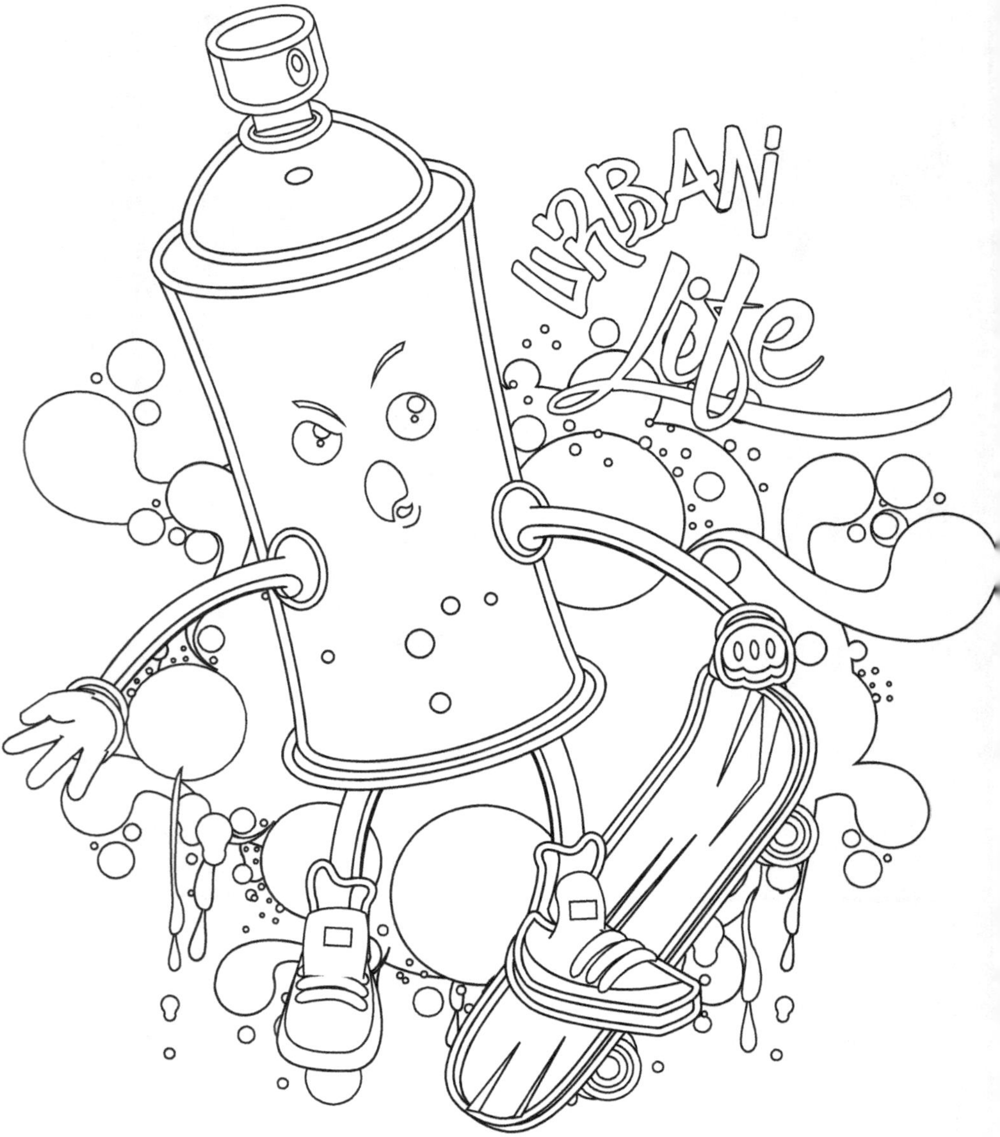
URBAN
Life

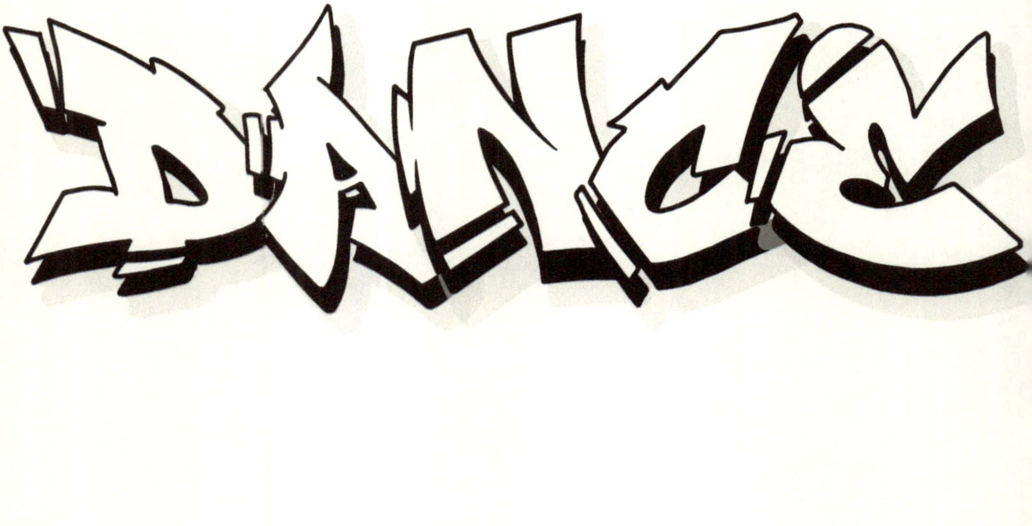
DANCE

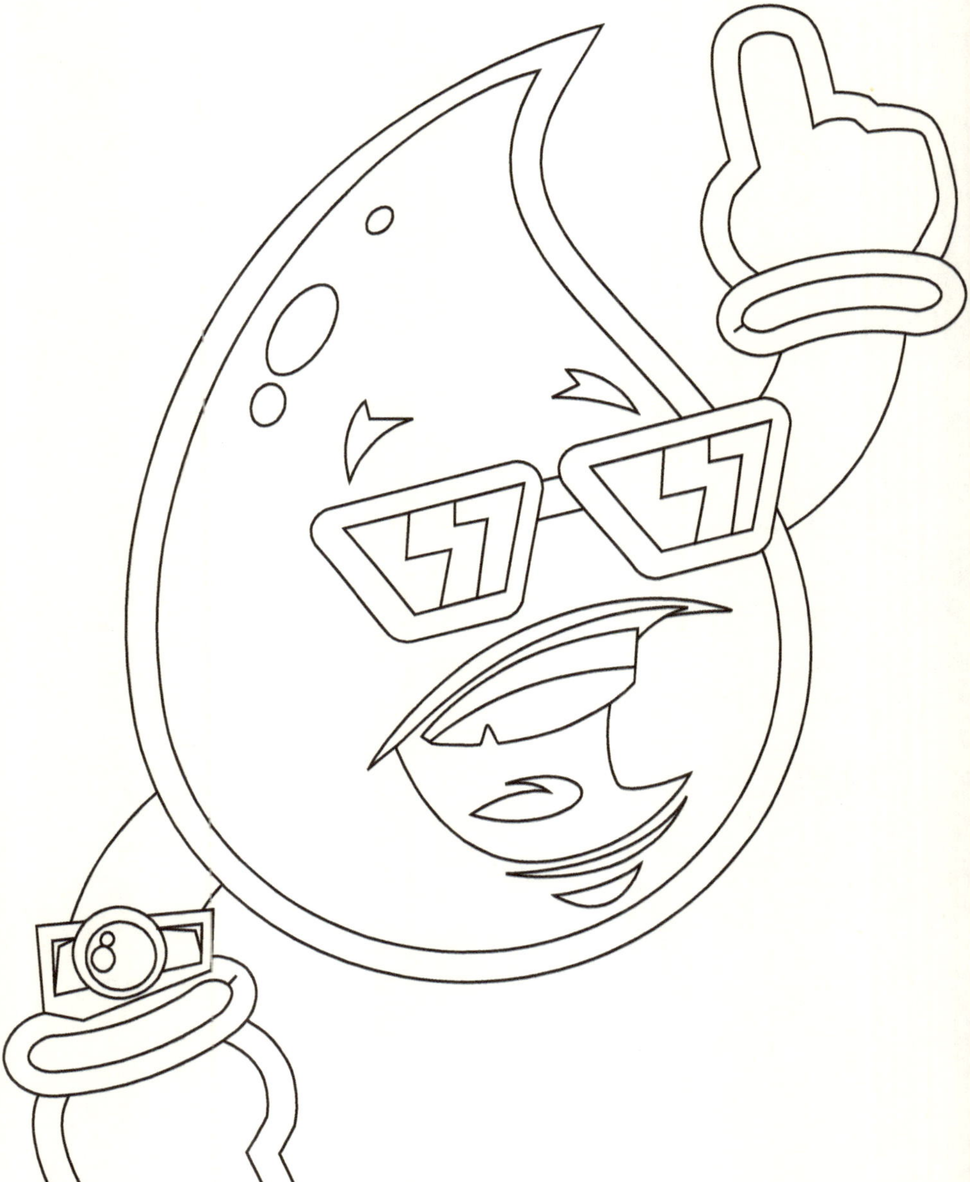

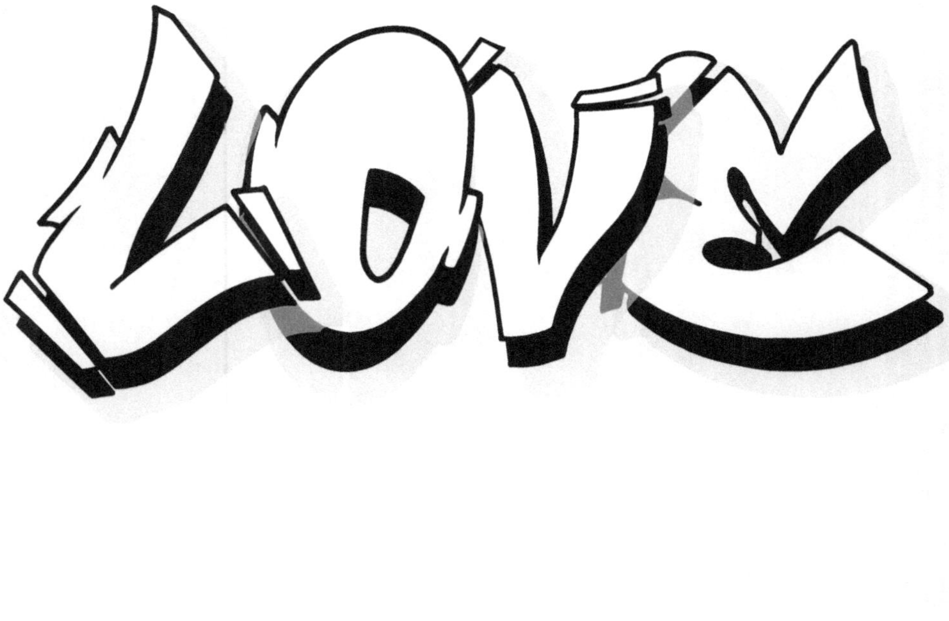
LOVE

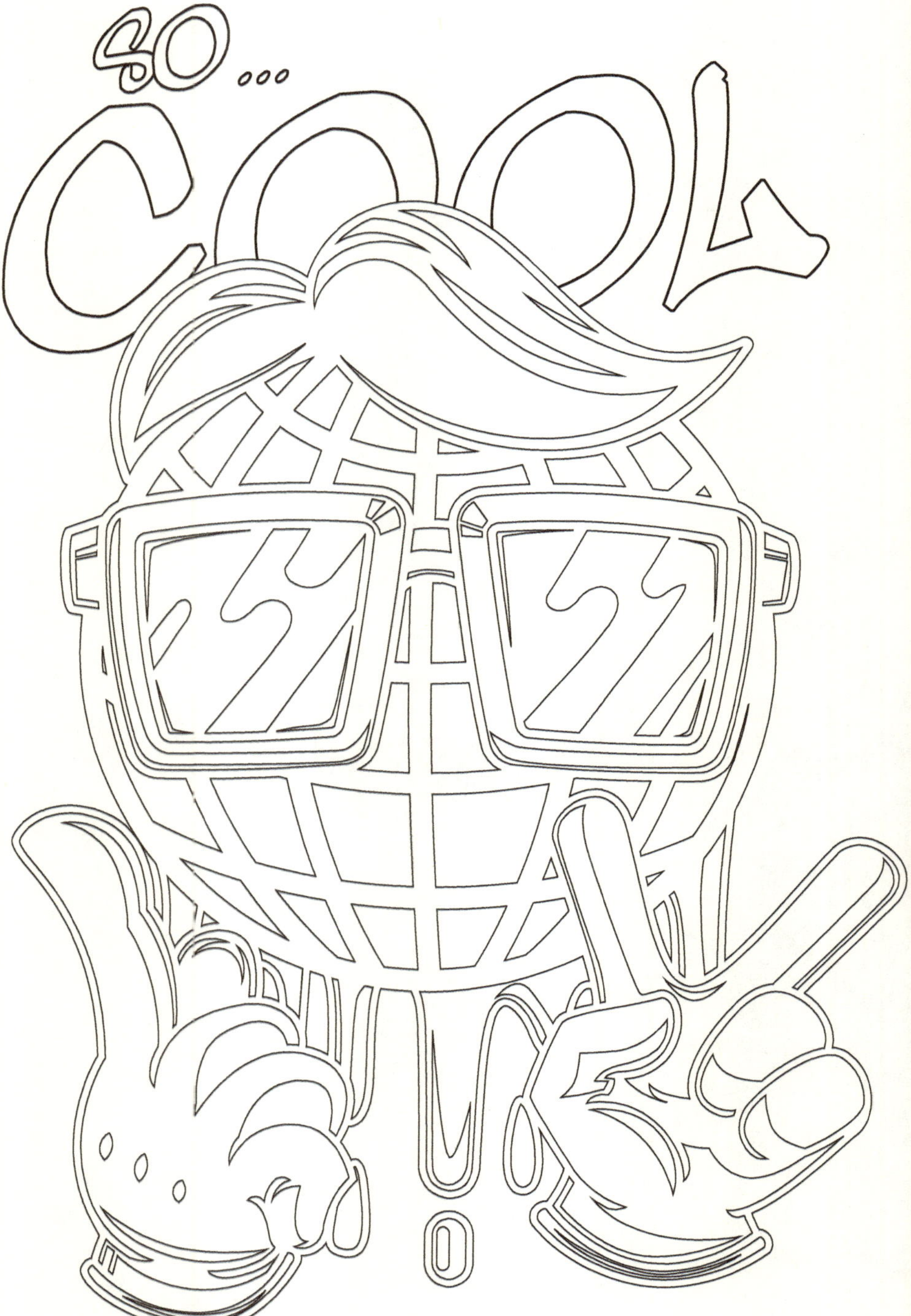
SO...
COOL

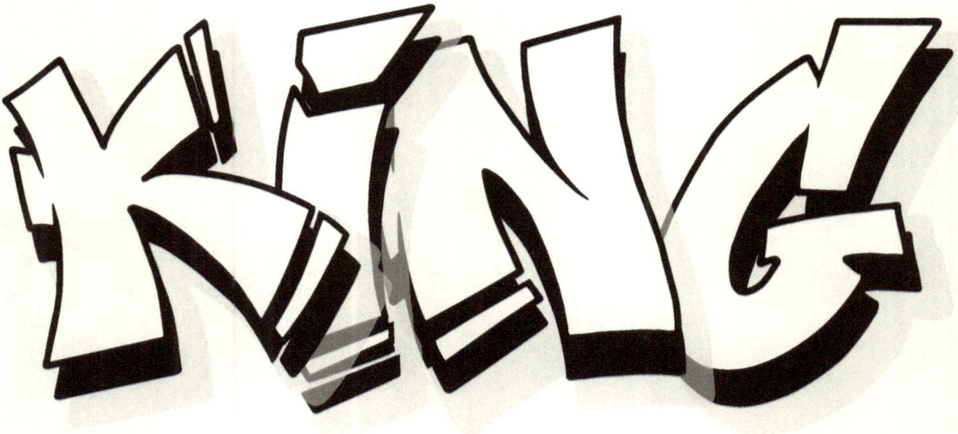
KING

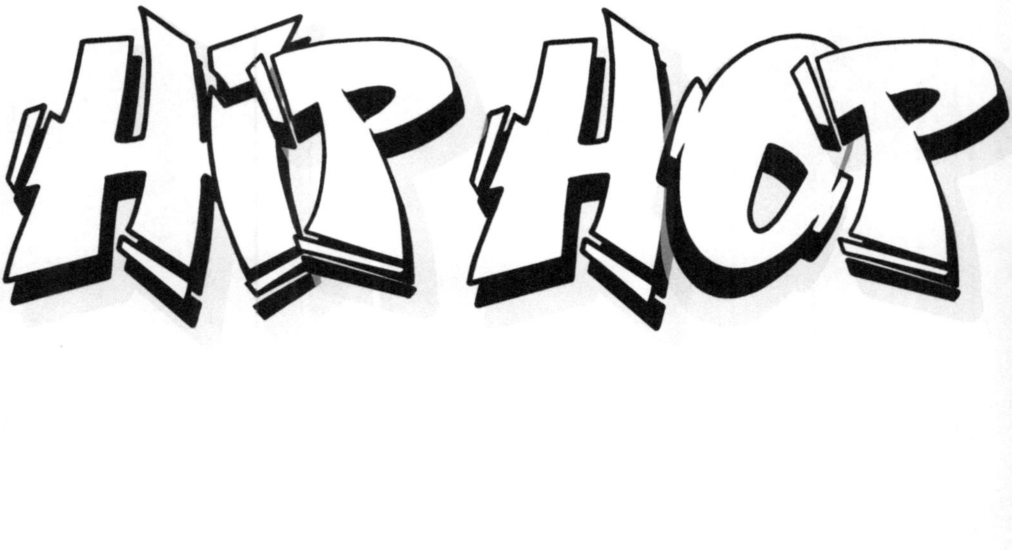
HIP HOP

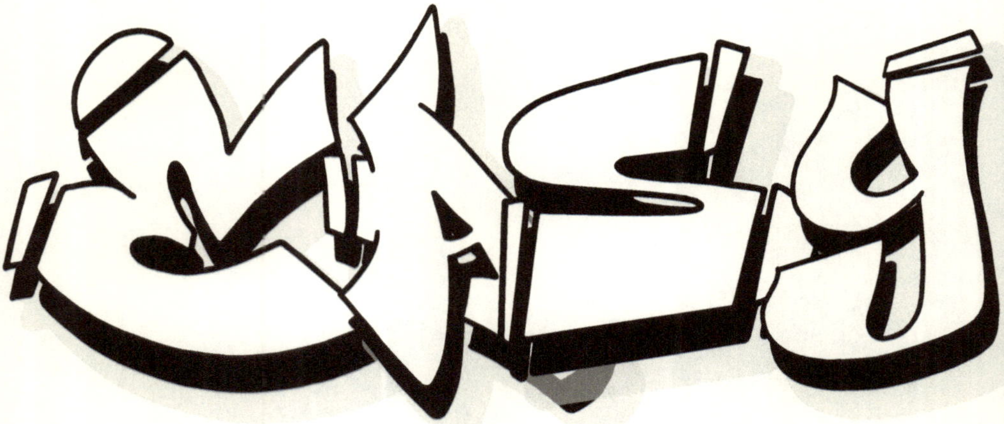

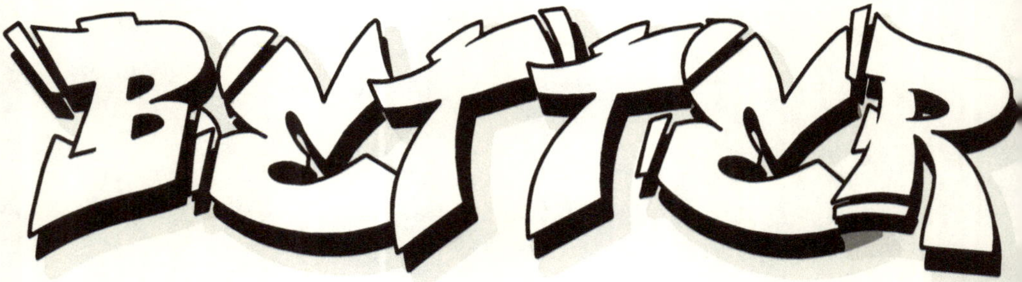
BETTER

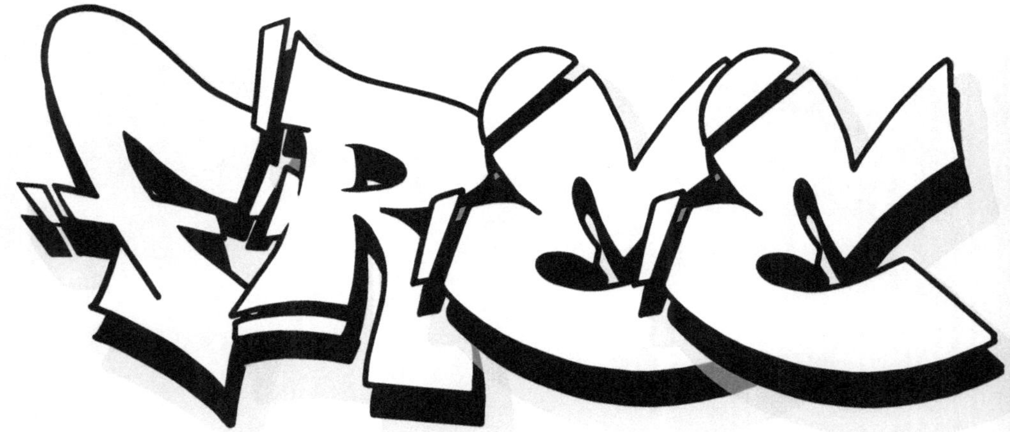

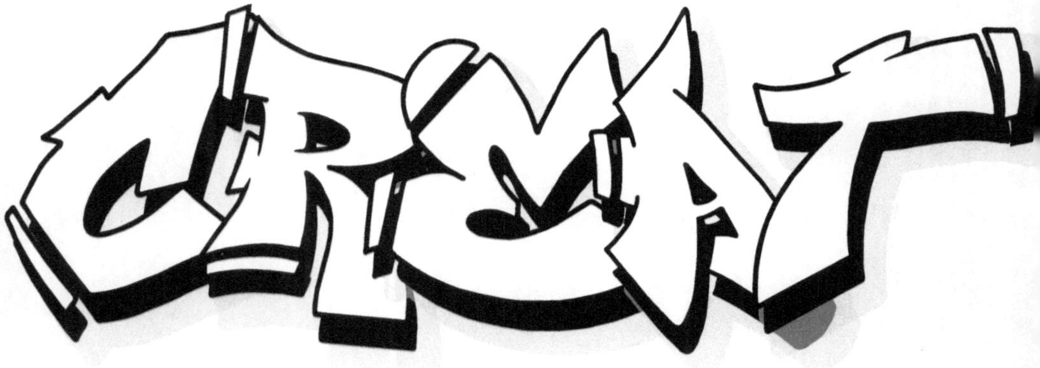

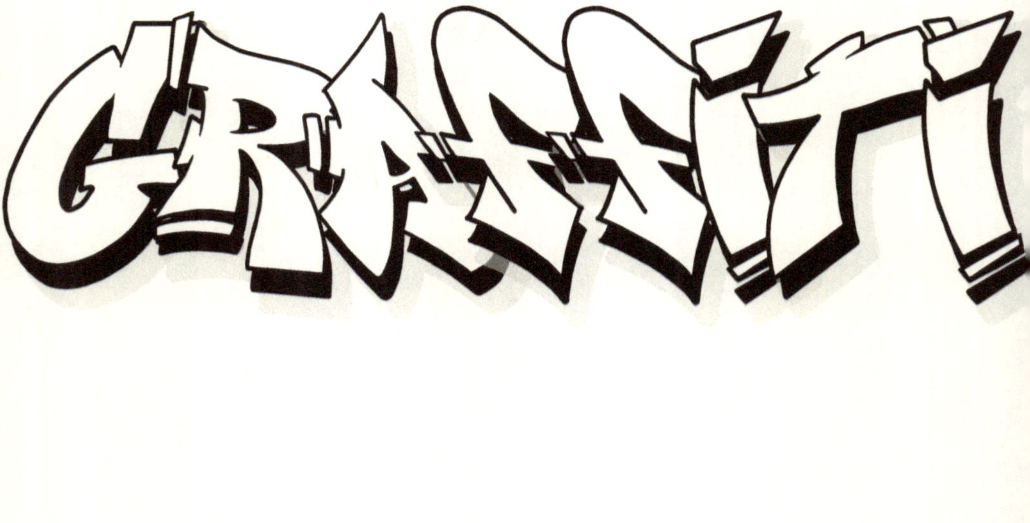
GRAFFITI

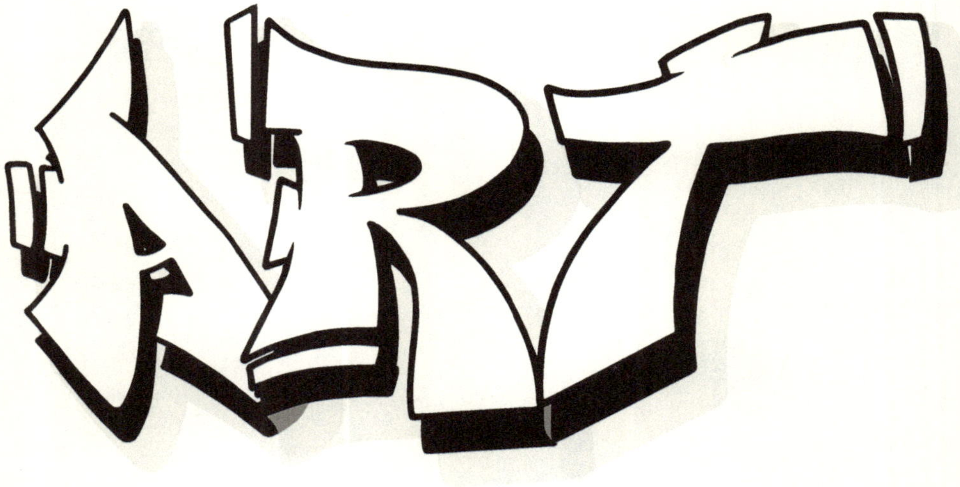
ART

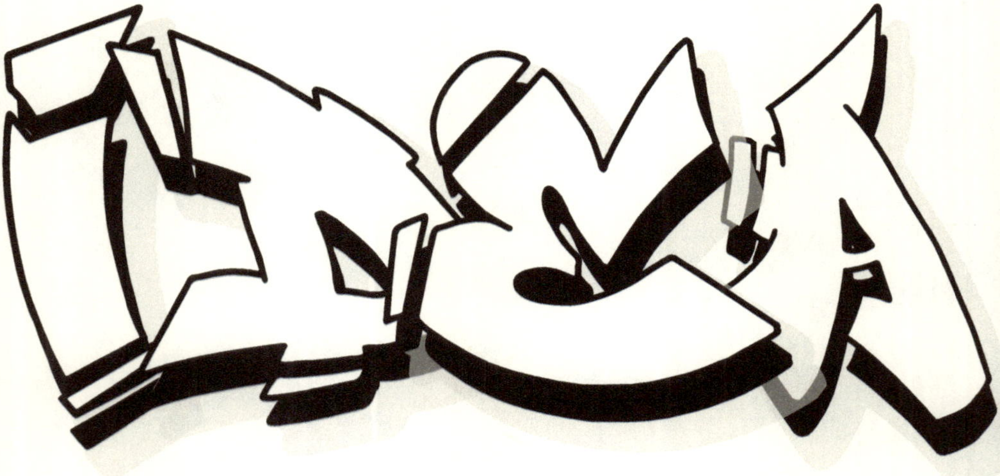

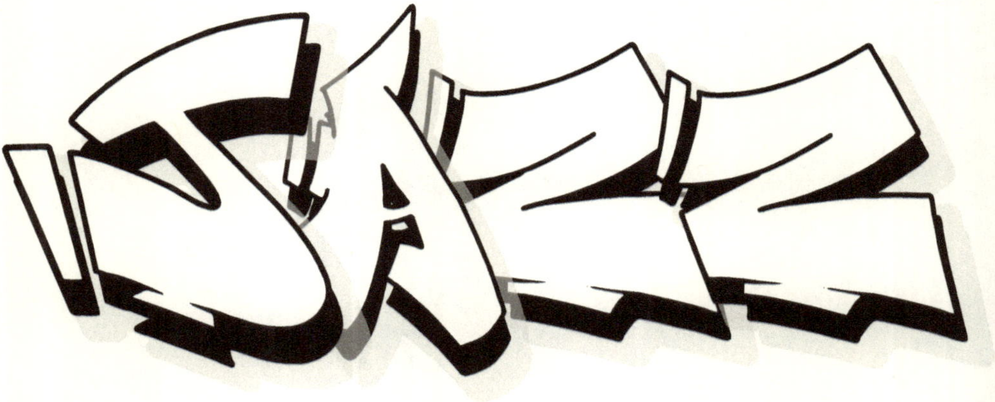
JAZZ

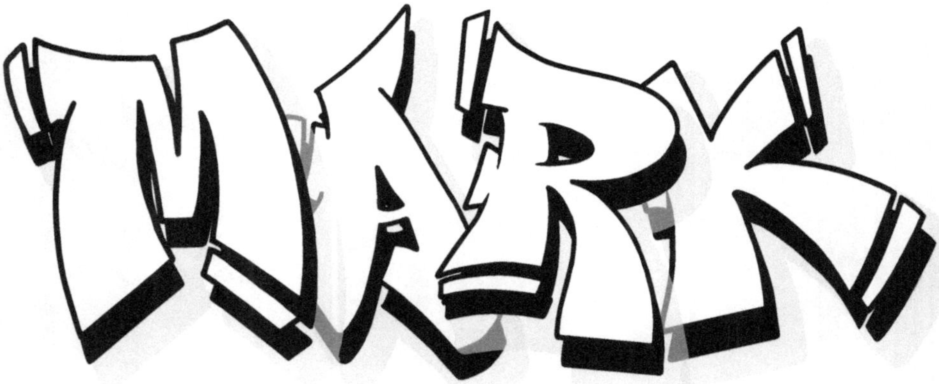
MARK

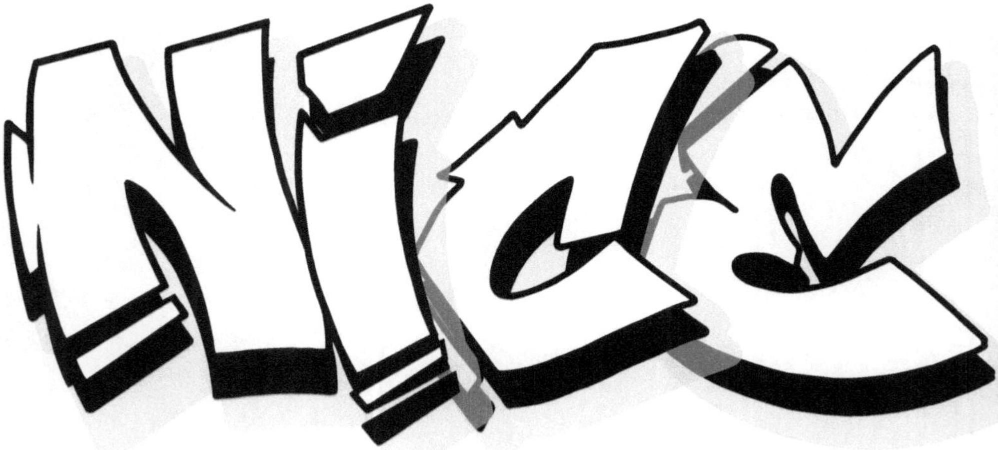
Nice

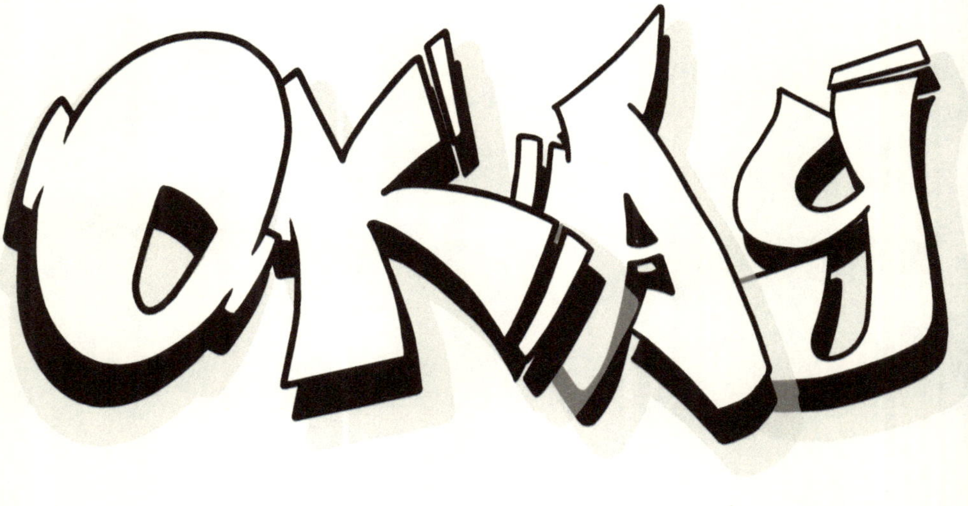
OKAY

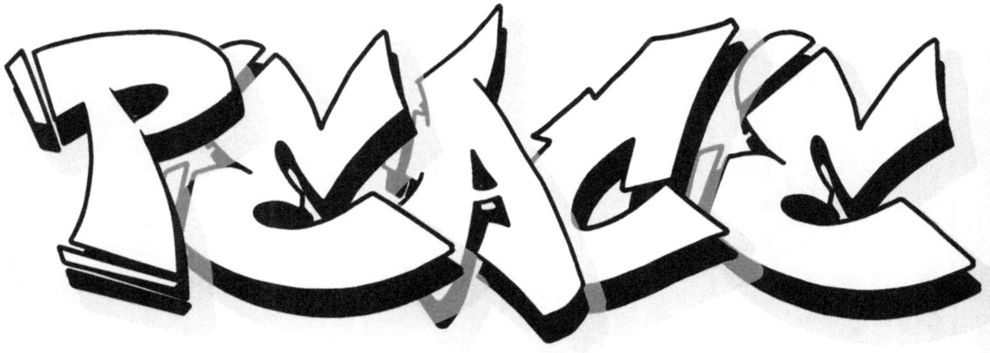
PEACE

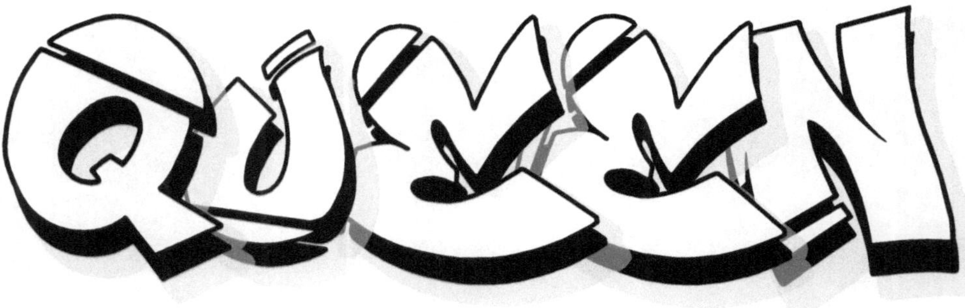
QUEEN

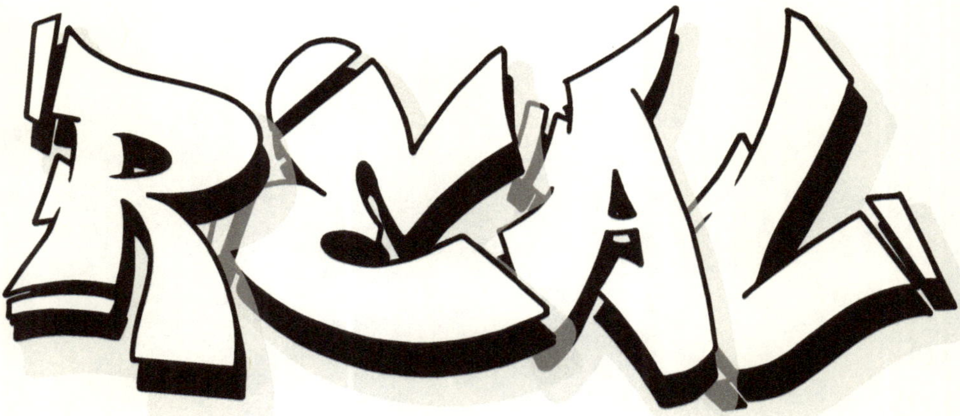
REAL

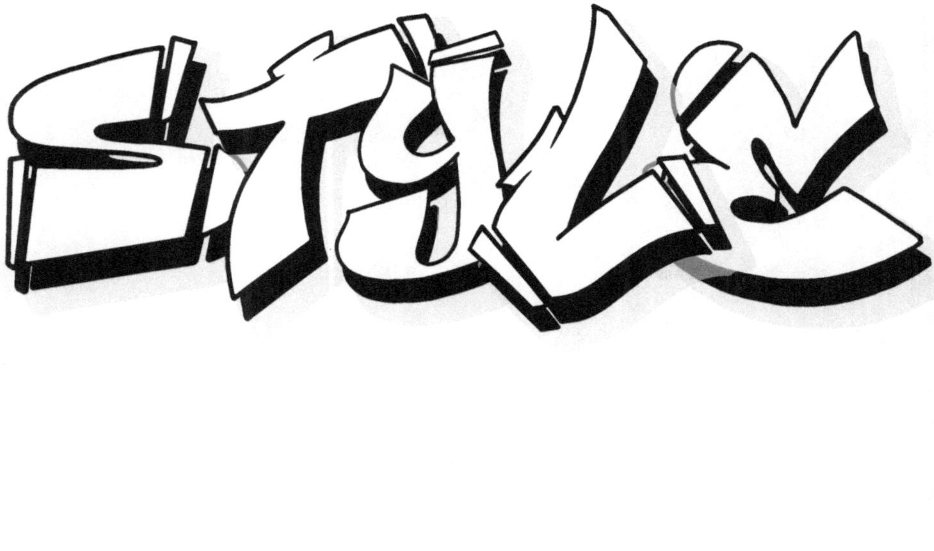
STYLE

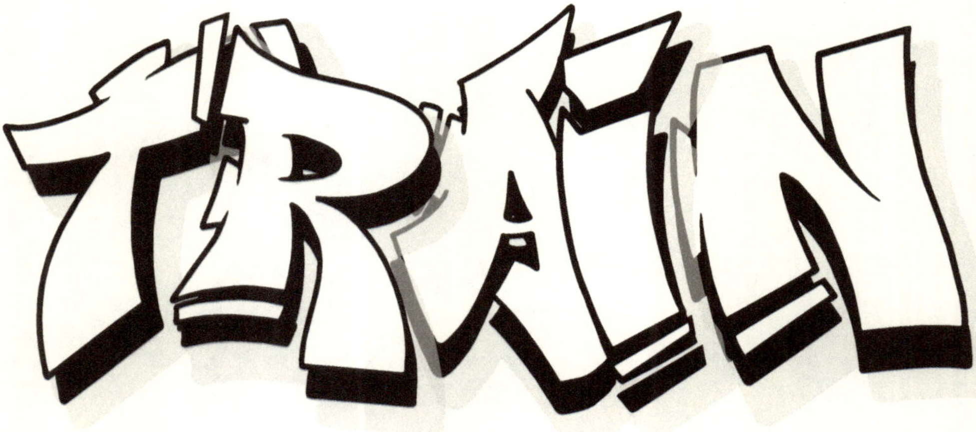
TRAIN

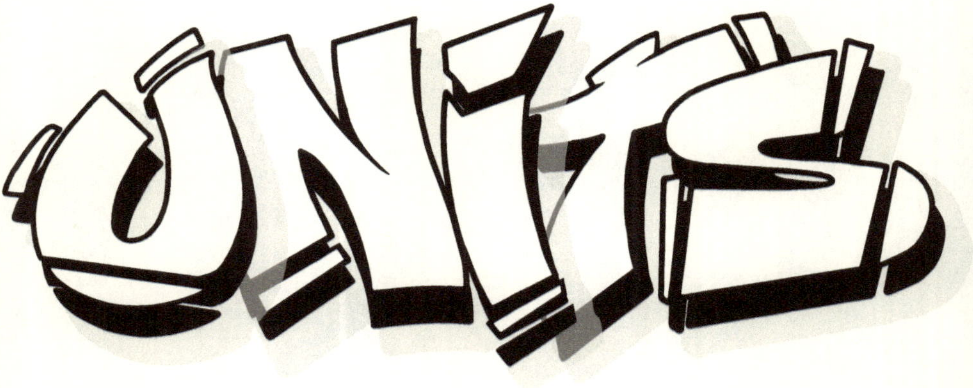
UNITS

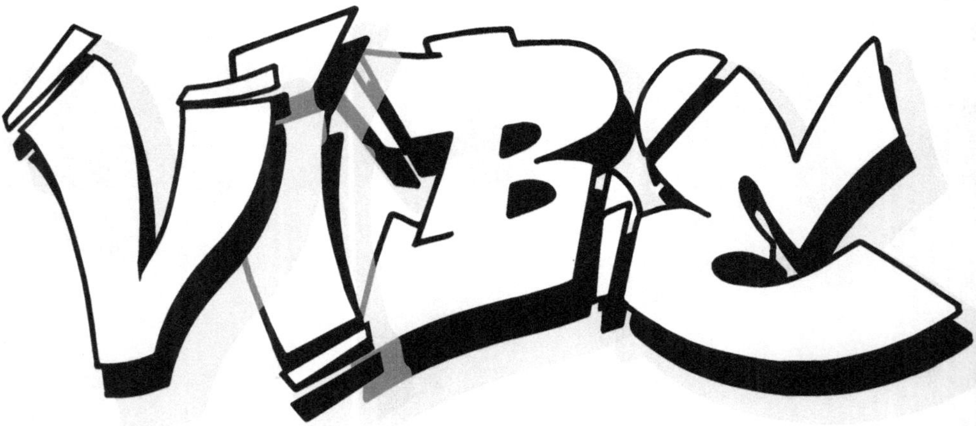

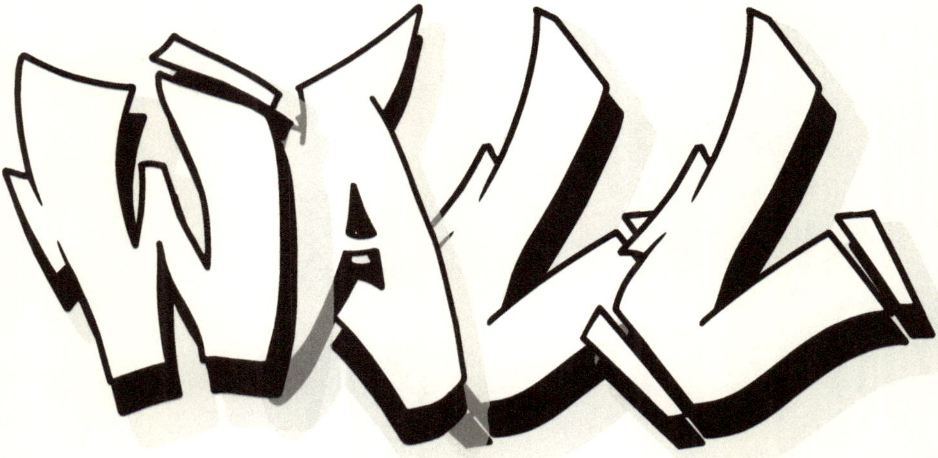
WALL

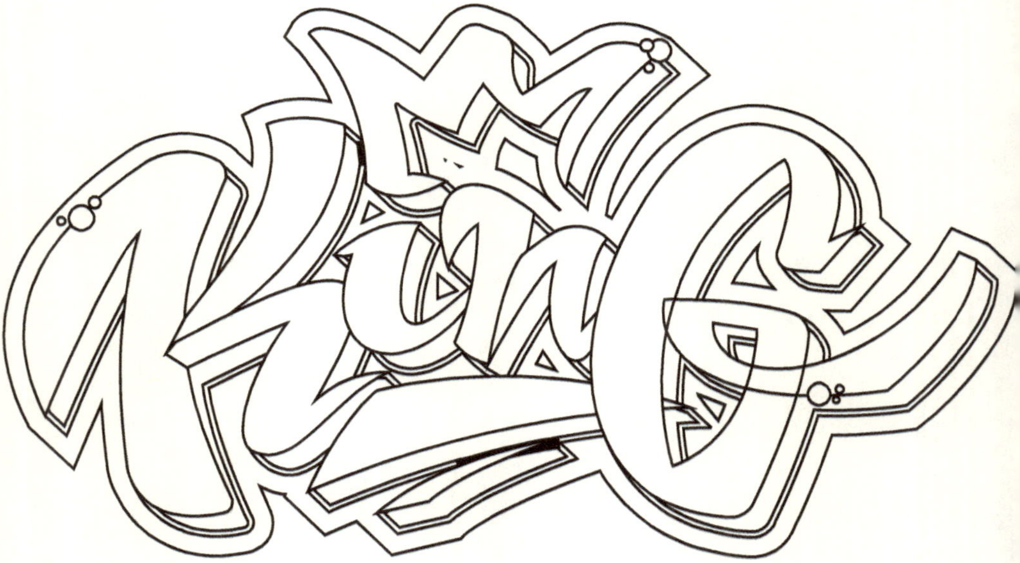
King

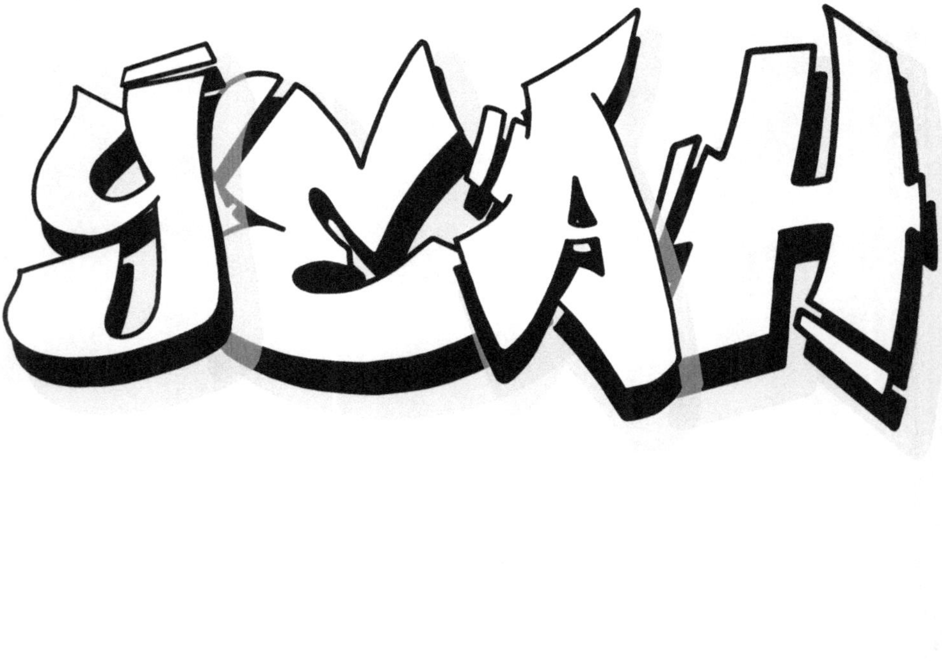
YEAH

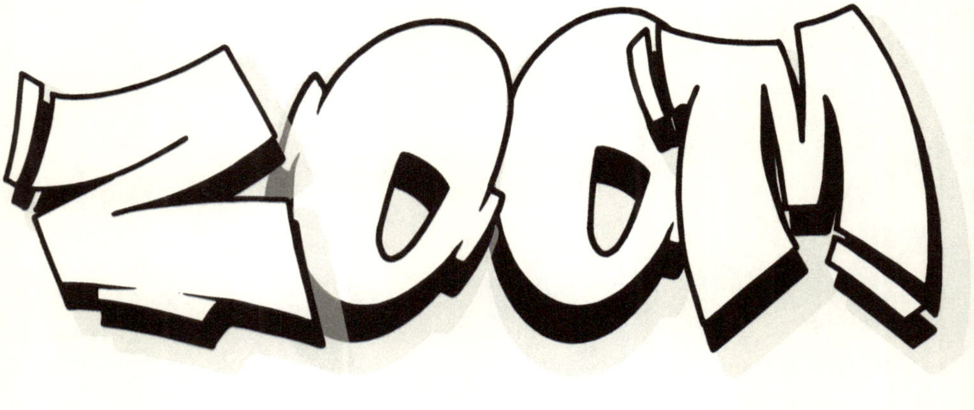
ZOOM

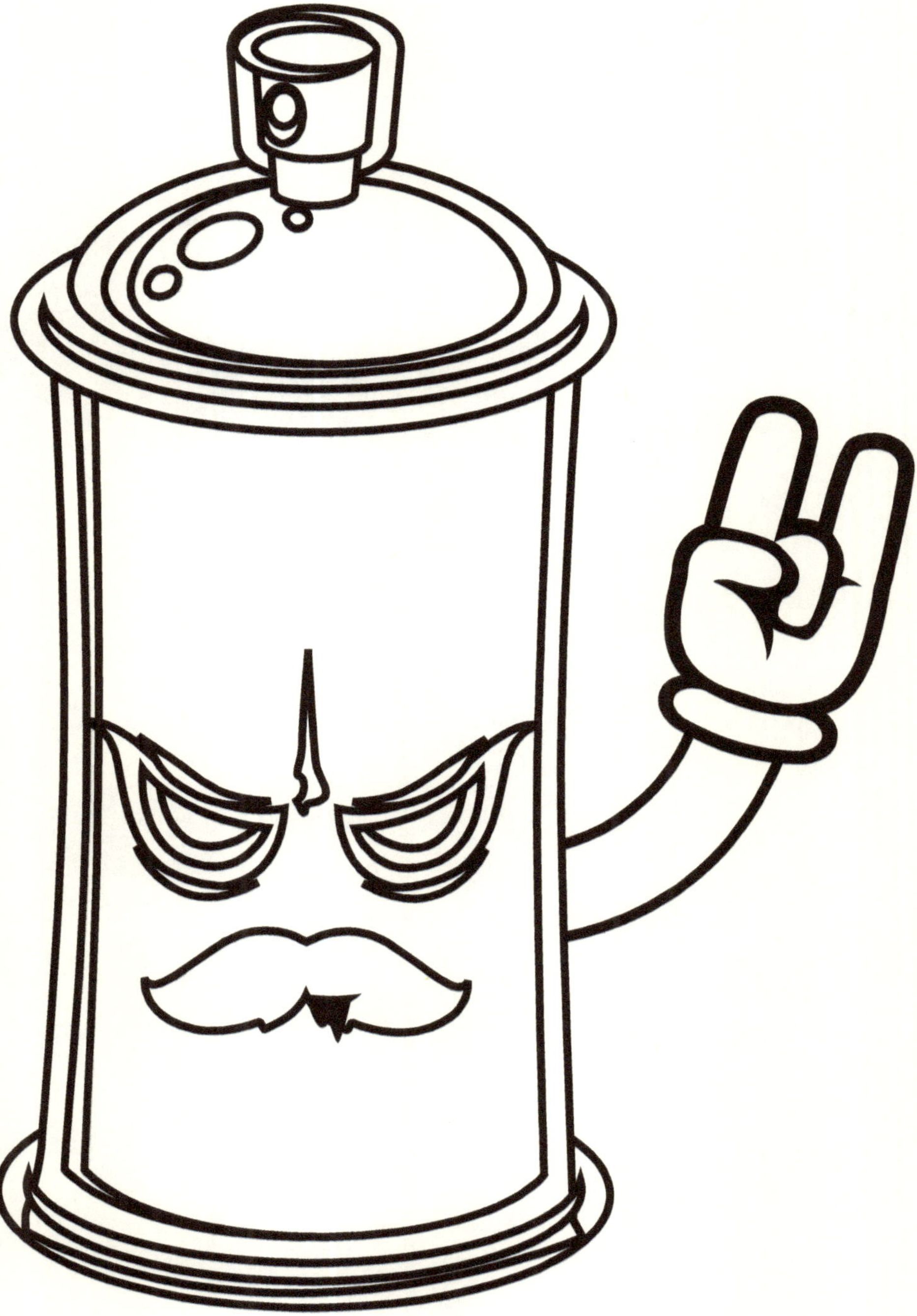

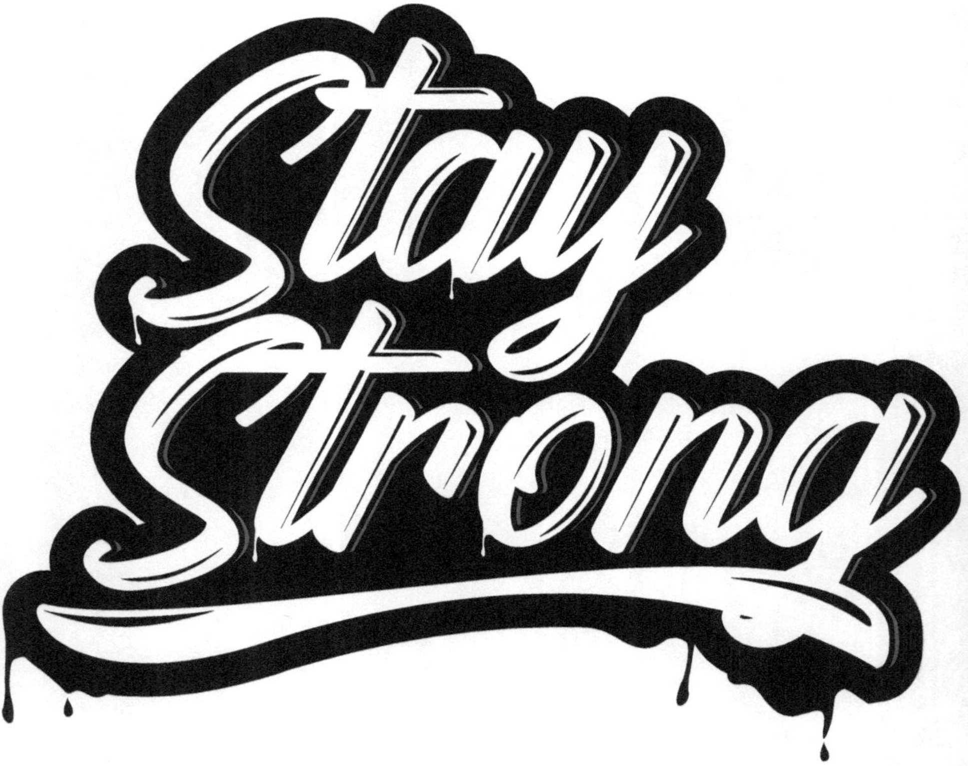
Stay
Strong

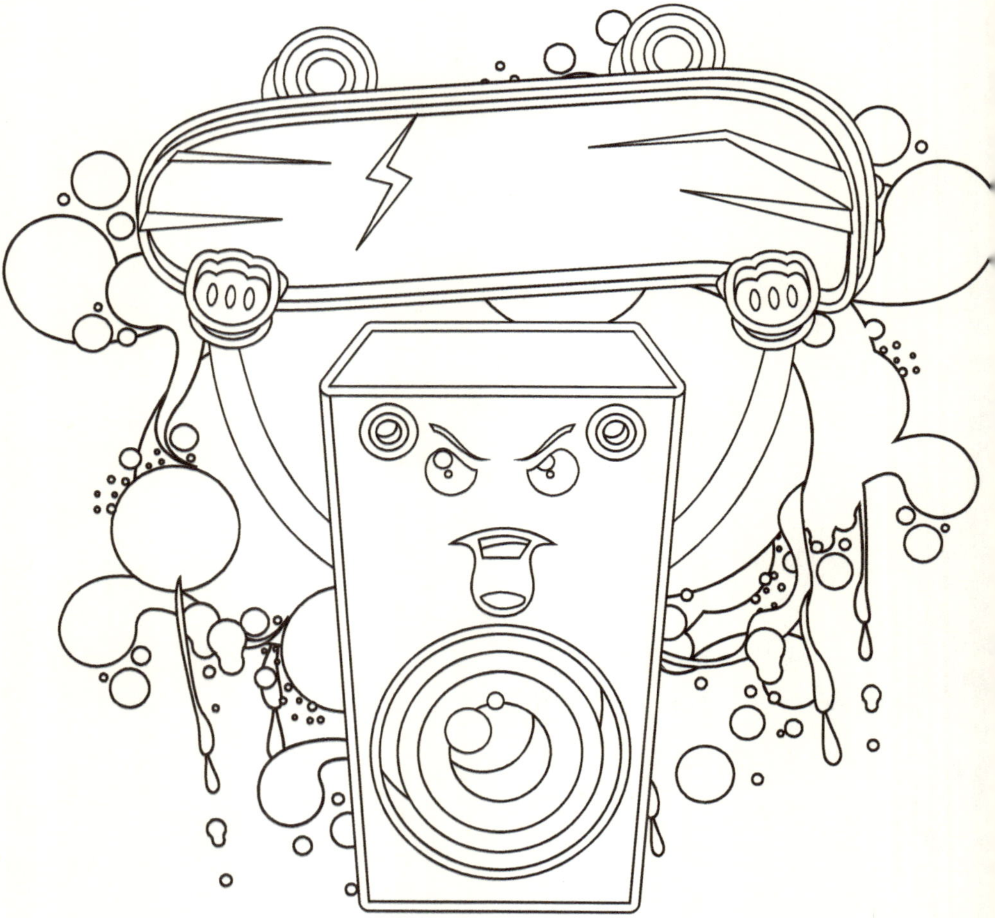

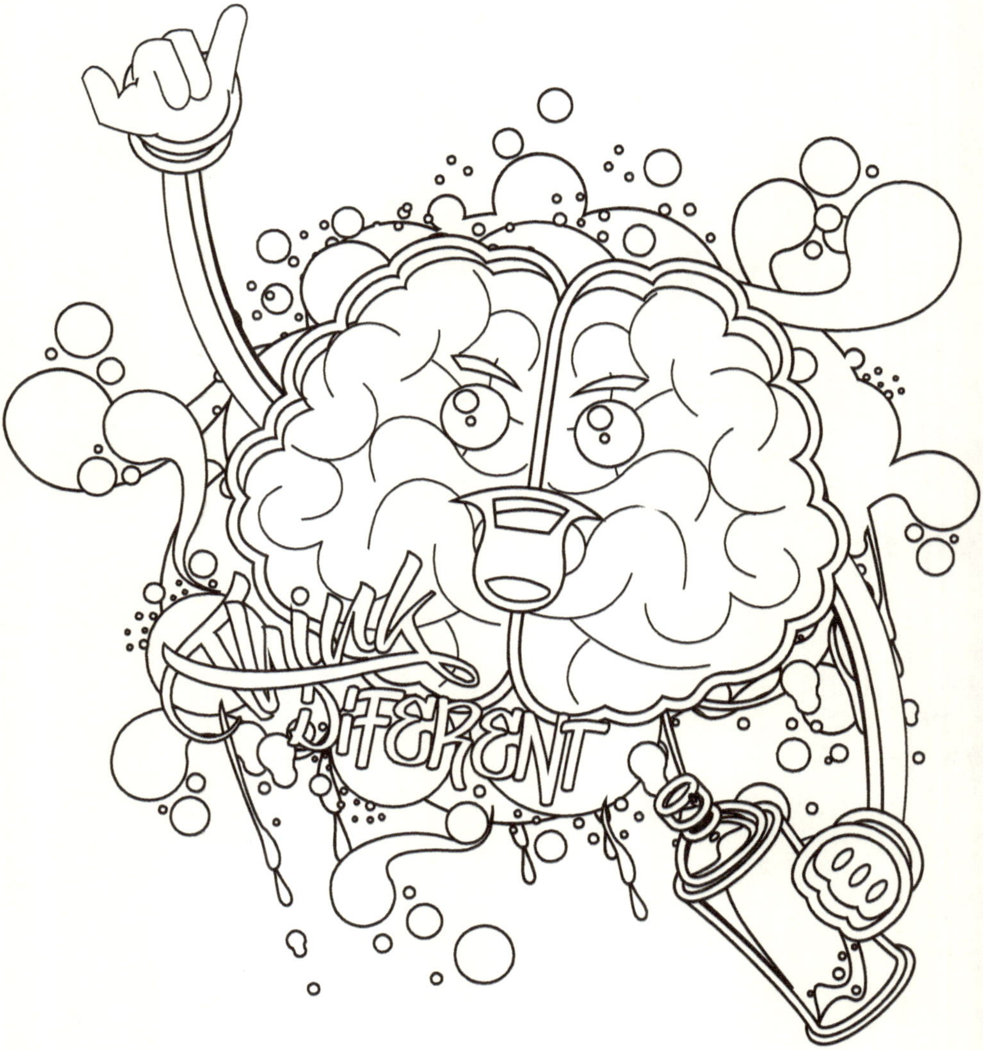
Think
DIFERENT

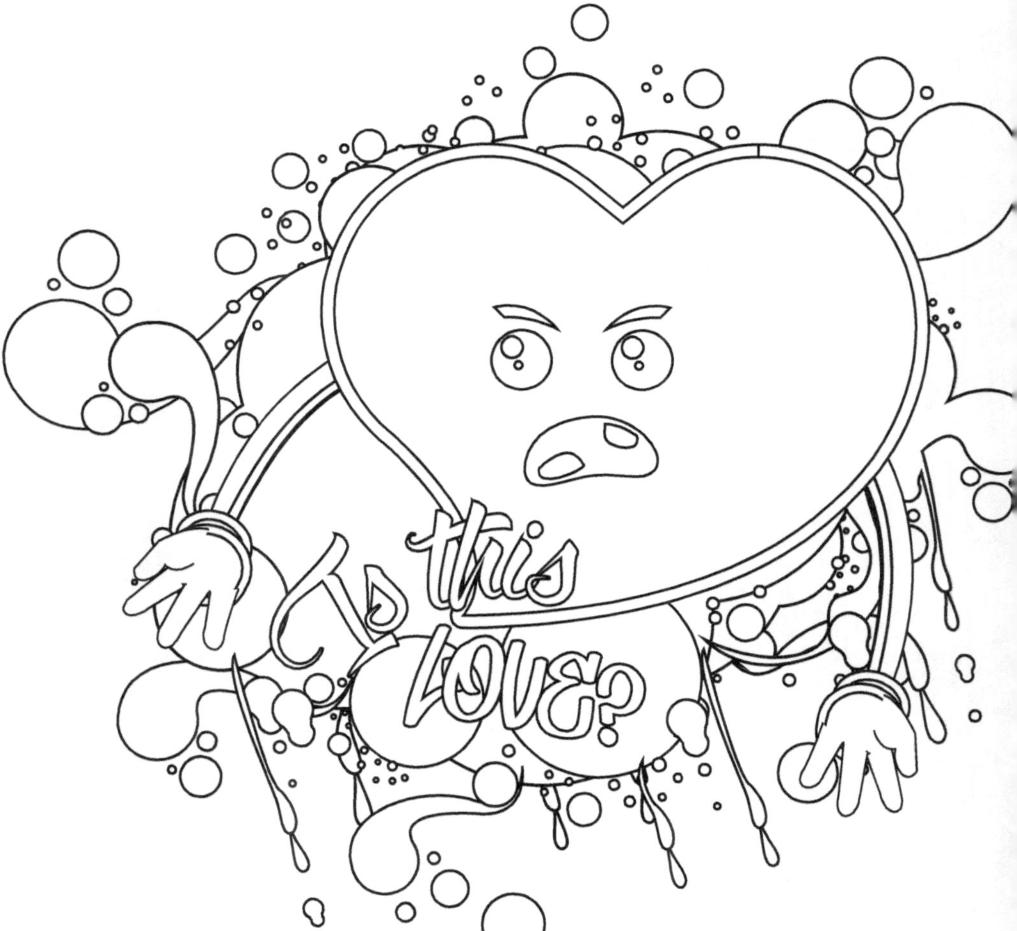
Is this
LOVE?

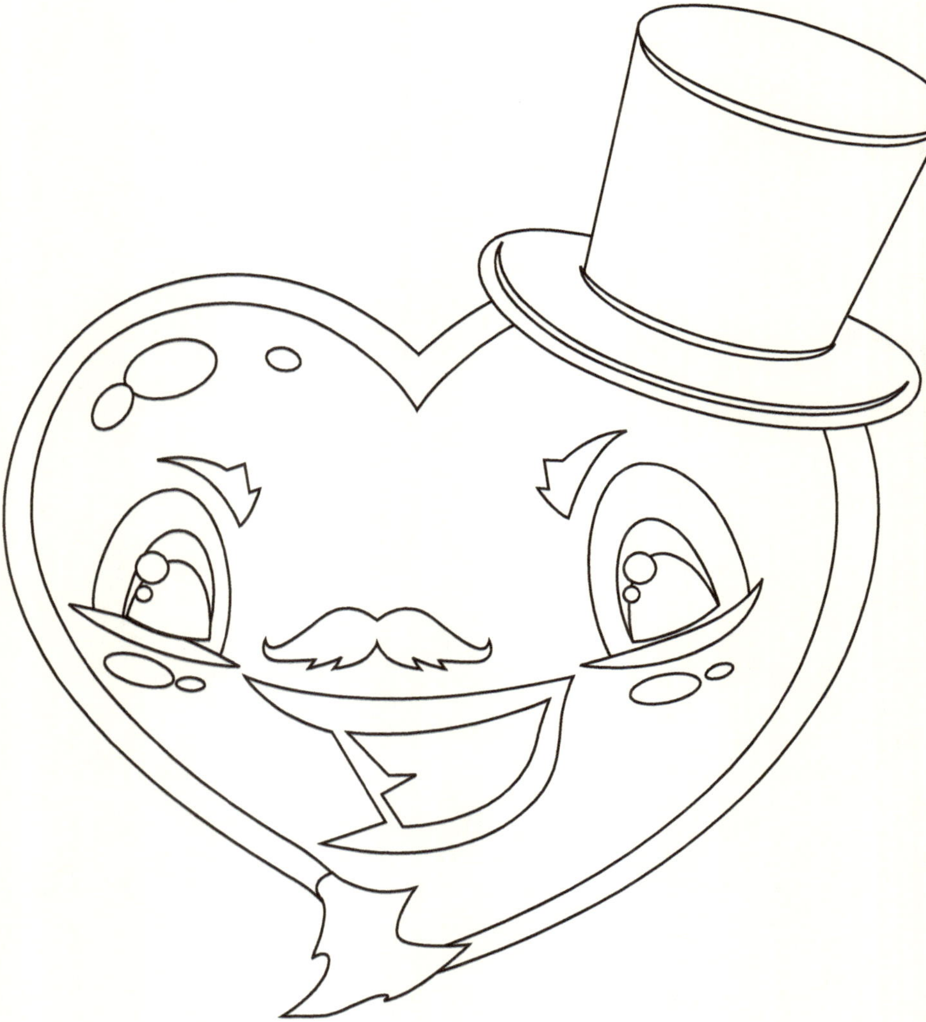

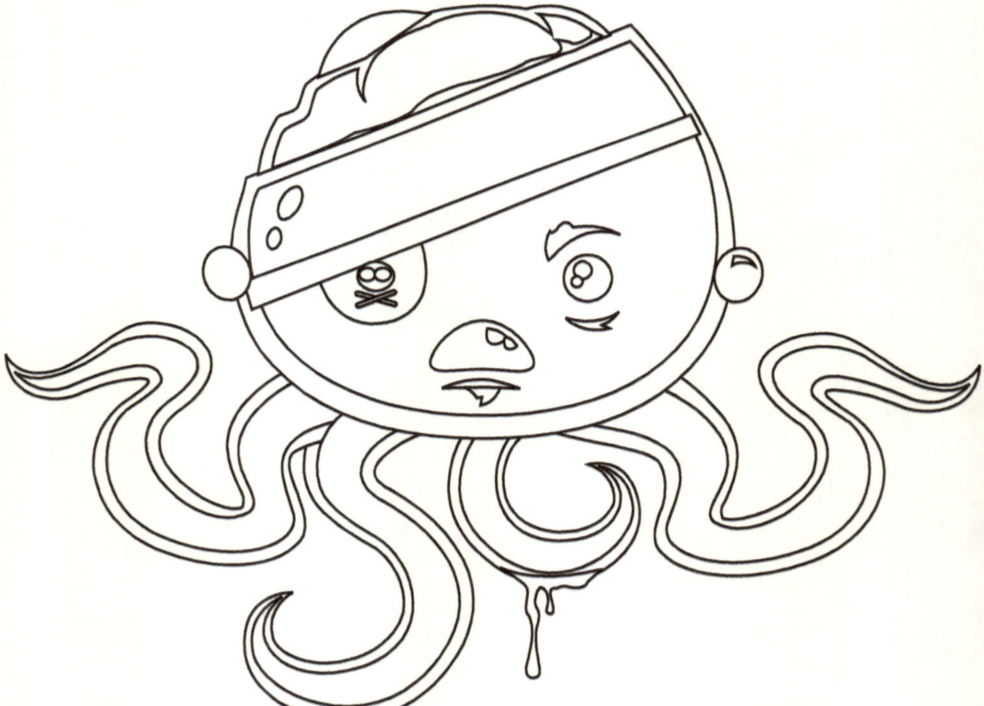

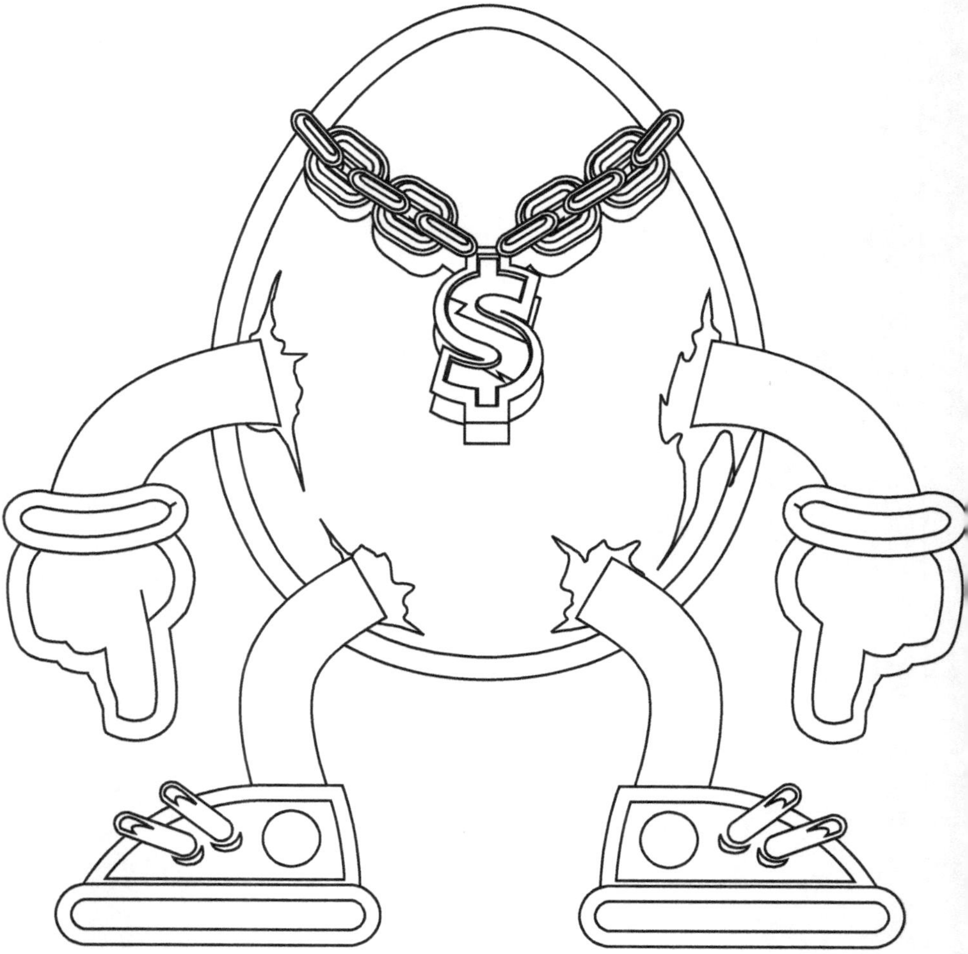

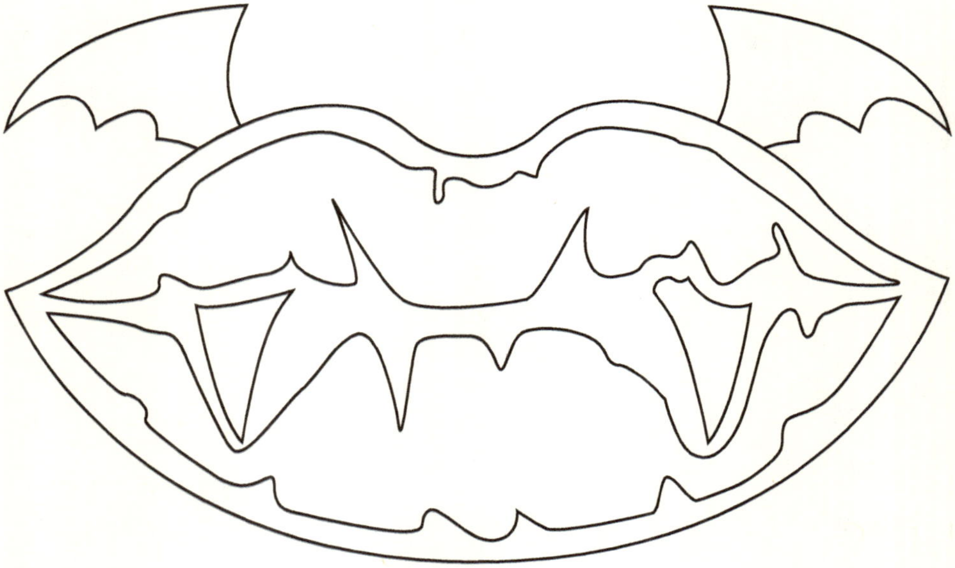

GOOD JOB

www.ingramcontent.com/pod-product-compliance
Lightning Source LLC
Chambersburg PA
CBHW020608220526
45463CB00006B/2507
* 9 7 9 8 6 5 4 0 1 6 1 7 1 *